Library of Congress Cataloging-in-Publication Data
Names: Lithgow, John, 1945- author.
Title: Trumpty Dumpty wanted a crown : verses for a despotic age / John Lithgow.
Other titles: Verses for a despotic age
Description: San Francisco : Chronicle Prism, [2020] | Series: Dumpty ; 1 |
Identifiers: LCCN 2020029056 | ISBN 9781797209463 (hardcover) | ISBN 9781797209487 (ebook)
Subjects: LCSH: Trump, Donald, 1946---Humor. | Trump, Donald, 1946---Caricatures and cartoons. | Trump, Donald, 1946---Poetry. | Political satire, American. | Humorous poetry, American. | American wit and humor. | United States--Politics and government--2017---Humor.
Classification: LCC E913.3 .L583 2020 | DDC 973.933092--dc23
LC record available at https://lccn.loc.gov/2020029056

Manufactured in the United States of America.

Illustrations by John Lithgow.
Design by Sara Schneider.
Typeset in Adobe Caslon, Brandon Grotesque, and Daft Brush.

10 9 8 7 6 5 4 3 2 1

Chronicle books and gifts are available at special quantity discounts to corporations, professional associations, literacy programs, and other organizations. For details and discount information, please contact our premiums department at corporatesales@chroniclebooks.com or at 1-800-759-0190.

CHRONICLE PRISM

Chronicle Prism is an imprint of Chronicle Books LLC,
680 Second Street, San Francisco, California 94107
chronicleprism.com

TRUMPTY DUMPTY
WANTED A CROWN

VERSES FOR A DESPOTIC AGE

JOHN LITHGOW

Author of the
NEW YORK TIMES BESTSELLER *DUMPTY*

CHRONICLE PRISM

"When somebody's the president of the United States, the authority is total, and that's the way it's got to be."

DUMPTY, APRIL 13, 2020

CONTENTS

Introduction: Just Yesterday 7

Trumpty Dumpty Wanted a Crown 11

Rabid Rudy 12

Fake News 15

The Tortoise and the Hare 17

O'Moluments 21

Cipollone's Fine Baloney 22

Rab-a-Dab-Dan 23

Counselor Jay 27

Twinkle, Twinkle, Kenneth Starr 29

Quiet Elaine 32

Bill, Barr the Door! 34

Rueful Roger 37

Our Substitute Science Teacher 40

Dumpty's Dolls 42

The Buckeye Firecracker 45

Trumpty Dumpty Wanted a Rout 48

Scoundrels and Heroes:
Limericks from the Seat of Government 50

A Requiem Scored for Kazoo 62

One Lucky Bastard...66

The Special Ops of Erik Prince 68

Diplomatic Gas 70

Recipe for Disaster 73

Reetle-Deet-Deet...76

Fire Bright!..78

The Invisible Man..80

A Pandemic's a Terrible Thing to Waste..........................82

Rah! Rah! Rah!..87

The Torys, or The Tiger King..89

Joe McCarthy's Lullaby...99

Our Witch Doctor in Chief... 101

Trumpty Dumpty Wanted a Title 102

Introduction

JUST YESTERDAY

Yesterday, some crazy stuff happened in Washington, DC. Remember?

In the midst of a raging pandemic, and after four straight days of nationwide protest against systemic racism and police brutality, President Donald Trump delivered a lacerating speech at the White House. He called himself "your law-and-order president" and threatened to use American military force against Americans. While he spoke, the sound of flash grenades and horses could be heard in the background as a hastily assembled army of federal, state, and local law enforcement cleared a crowd of peaceful demonstrators from Lafayette Square.

Immediately after his speech, the president strutted through the cleared-out park with a gaggle of his top officials dumbly trotting along behind him. Taking several of them by surprise, he posed with a Bible for a photo op in front of St. John's Church. He then summoned a few of the officials to stand beside him for more photos. They included his rumpled attorney general, his bewildered defense secretary, and his perky new press secretary. They looked like hapless audience members hauled up onstage by Dame Edna to make them look foolish in front of the crowd.

It was a scene of autocratic sham glamour that would not have been out of place in a modern-day retelling of "The Emperor's New Clothes." King Dumpty's winsome daughter had carried the Bible to the photo op in a $1,540 Max Mara handbag.

Much of the country thought this political charade was crass, infuriating, and deeply disturbing. Even Trump's most fervent supporters must have thought it was a really bad idea.

I thought it was all those things, but I also thought it was stupid and ridiculous. If it weren't such a horror show, it would have been farce.

What a poem it would have made for this book!

Alas, all of this happened just yesterday, on June 1, 2020. My poems had already been completed and sent off to my publisher just days before.

So much for comic timing.

With political satire, timing is everything, and the cumbersome process of book publishing makes timing especially tricky. I wrote the following verses in real time, responding to events as they occurred. But with events coming at me with such speed and impact, I was faced with a harsh truth: Everything I write on one day is ancient history on the next. With the lag between completing my poems and having them see the light of day, four months of history goes unaddressed.

Writing this book has made me think a lot about history. In fact, it's my second book of Trump-era poems in the course of a year. The first, called simply *Dumpty*, was published in October of 2019. When it appeared, a surprising thing kept happening. Over and over, readers would remark that they had forgotten all about the targets of many of the poems. These were figures who had flamed out early in the Trump administration: Tom Price, Scott Pruitt, Ronny Jackson, and many more.

It turns out that my smart-ass poems had performed a minor but important service: They had reminded readers of forgotten moments in our recent history and, by the handy device of rhyme, had made them a little more memorable. So now, as I think about my intentions with this second book, I realize they are threefold: to make you laugh, to make you mad, and to make you remember.

As you read the following poems, you'll come across one of my favorites. It's called "Fake News." It concludes with the following couplet, in the voice of our president himself:

Fake news doesn't bother me.
I'll just rewrite history.

These poems are my modest attempt to make sure that doesn't happen.

JL, June 2, 2020

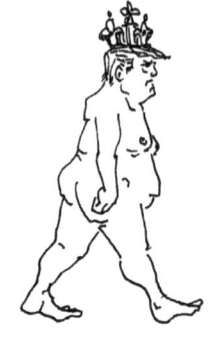

TRUMPTY DUMPTY WANTED A CROWN

Trumpty Dumpty wanted a crown
To make certain he never would have to step down.
He wanted a robe made of ermine and velvet.
The Constitution? He wanted to shelve it.

With impeachment a wash, his ambition had grown.
He wanted an orb, a scepter, a throne;
Six royal palaces, six royal carriages,
A church dispensation for six royal marriages;

Courtiers installed on his own Supreme Court
And royal beheadings, if only for sport.
He craved the occasional royal procession
And *(gasp!)* the eventual royal succession.

Trumpty Dumpty gets his way
Unless the public has something to say.
If we let him have all of his favorite things,
We'll have to endure the divine right of kings.

On December 18, 2019, **DONALD J. TRUMP** *became the third American president to be impeached. Alleged to have used the levers of government to solicit help from Ukraine for his reelection, he was charged with abuse of power and obstruction of Congress. The Republican-majority Senate acquitted him of both charges.*

RABID RUDY

What goes on with Rabid Rudy,
Monster of ineptitudy?
Dumpty's spinning weather vane
Botched his mission in Ukraine.
Mixing bribes and dirty tricks,
He soiled our geopolitics.
Filled with rage and babbling bluster,
"America's Mayor" has lost his luster.

During the impeachment inquiry, Donald Trump denied allegations that he sent his personal attorney **RUDY GIULIANI** *to Ukraine to investigate his political opponents. In February 2020, after his acquittal, Trump admitted to sending Giuliani to Ukraine.*

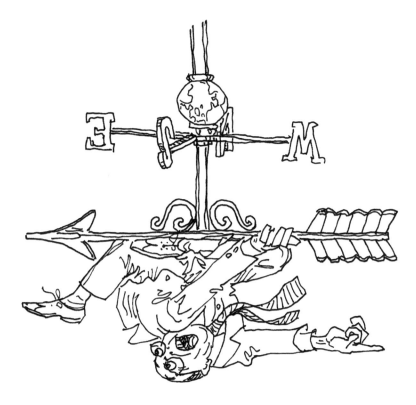

FAKE NEWS

People say that heretofore
I kept Black tenants from my door
Using legal trickery,
But fake news doesn't bother me.

They say that falsifying facts is
How I skirted all my taxes.
People call it larceny,
But fake news doesn't bother me.

Constantly I'm found at fault,
Charged with sexual assault,
Harassment, and adultery,
But fake news doesn't bother me.

Starving students, people say,
Had their futures ripped away
By Dumpty University,
But fake news doesn't bother me.

They smear me with the vilest things
Like payoffs for my casual flings
From the campaign treasury,
But fake news doesn't bother me.

People say I monetize
All my presidential ties,
Boosting my prosperity,
But fake news doesn't bother me.

They say my meddling in Ukraine
Left an ignominious stain
Tantamount to treachery,
But fake news doesn't bother me.

They say in days coronaviral
I propelled our downward spiral
Through my imbecility,
But fake news doesn't bother me.

Notwithstanding crimes like these,
I'll continue as I please.
Fake news doesn't bother me.
I'll just rewrite history.

Among other allegations, Donald Trump is said to have discriminated against African Americans as a New York real estate developer; committed tax fraud to avoid paying income tax on $50 million; engaged in sexual misconduct toward more than twenty-five women; endorsed Trump University's fraudulent scheme to target the uneducated and the elderly; used the power of his office to attempt blackmail in Ukraine; and mishandled the government's early response to the coronavirus pandemic.

THE TORTOISE AND THE HARE

Have you heard of the tale of the Tortoise and Hare,
That anthropomorphic political pair?
Their years of combative and bitter contention
Drew more than their share of the public's attention.

The Tortoise (named Mitch) was renowned for his guile,
The Senate majority's leading reptile,
While the Hare was a POTUS, a flashy young mammal
Whose smile was a sunbeam of gleaming enamel.

The quick-witted Hare (whose name was Barack)
Floated programs the Tortoise endeavored to block.
As fast as the Hare could devise and propose them,
The crusty old Tortoise would try to bulldoze them.

But the source of the Hare's most implacable grudges?
The Tortoise quashed all of his nominee judges.
One case made the Hare absolutely irate:
Merrick Garland, not even brought up for debate.

The Hare soon gave way to a rampaging swine
Whose politics followed the populist line.
Hence the Tortoise's tale took a different tack:
Stumping for Dumpty, the plump razorback.

Dumpty, of course, was a suitable match
For the boys in the Tortoise's tight kaffeeklatsch.
Together they moved with a speed unabated
To kibosh whatever the Hare had created.

And the Tortoise's prime legislative intent?
Lending justice a strict archconservative bent.
Gaming the process he played fast and loose,
Confirming new judges like shit through a goose.

Yet the crowning event of the Tortoise's story
Has brought him a measure of dubious glory,
Inscribing his name in our history's log:
The impeachment of Dumpty, the razorback hog.

By keeping his party in line and tight-knitted,
The Tortoise prevailed and got Dumpty acquitted.
But by treating the trial as a legal blood sport,
He rendered the Senate a kangaroo court.

The congressional doghouse will surely await
When the Tortoise embraces his ultimate fate.
While the Hare, whose enshrinement is nearly complete,
Will smile from his perch in the catbird seat.

Their tale, full of treachery, folly, and quarrel,
Leaves us at last with a practical moral:
Since power makes each of us history's pawn,
Use caution when choosing whose side you are on.

During the presidency of **BARACK OBAMA,** *Senate Majority Leader* **MITCH MCCONNELL** *blocked many of Obama's policies and judicial nominations. In early 2020, Senator McConnell led his party's successful effort to acquit President Donald Trump at his impeachment trial in the U.S. Senate.*

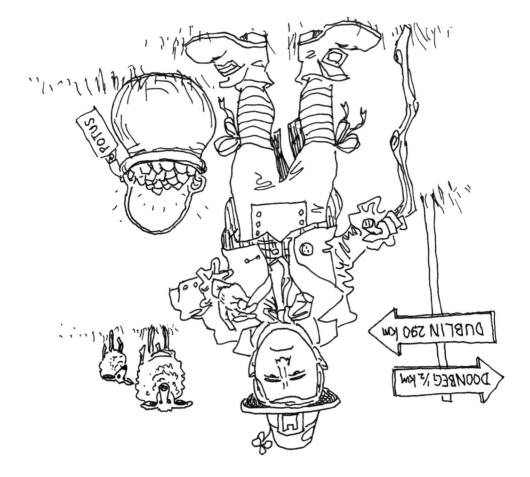

O'MOLUMENTS

U.S. airmen making merry
On a jaunt at Trump Turnberry;
Heads of state at Trump DC
Buying off the franchisee;
Trump proposing Trump Doral,
Cash his hidden rationale;
Doonbeg hosting Veep Mike Pence:
Did someone say "O'Moluments"?

*Donald Trump's official duties have often been entangled
with his privately owned corporations: In August 2019, Trump
suggested that the next G7 summit of world leaders be hosted at
his golf resort in Doral, Florida; throughout his term, American
military have stayed at Trump Turnberry, his luxury resort in
Scotland; and in September 2019, Vice President* **MIKE PENCE**
*stayed at Trump's Doonbeg Resort in Ireland, 181 miles from his
official meetings.*

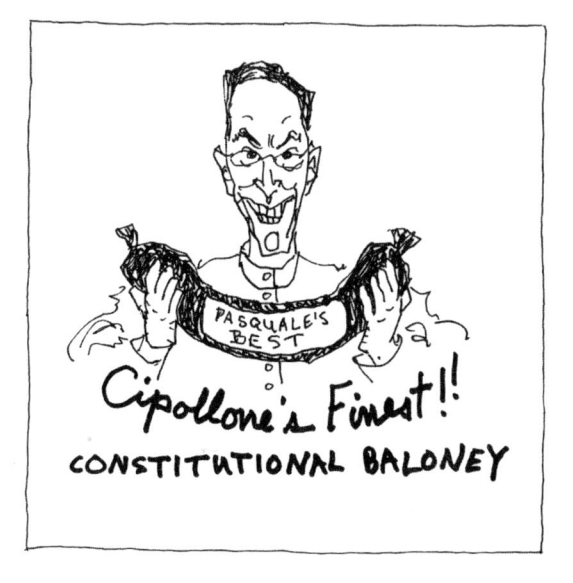

CONSTITUTIONAL BALONEY

CIPOLLONE'S FINE BALONEY

Here's another Dumpty crony,
Crafty snake with heart of stony,
Spouting constitutional baloney
From the foot of Dumpty's throney.
Up 'til now a rank unknowny:
Meet Pasquale Cipollone!

As White House Counsel for President Donald Trump,
PASQUALE "PAT" CIPOLLONE *blended political bias and
rhetoric to attack House leaders' approach to Trump's impeachment,
claiming that the impeachment process set forth in the Constitution
is unconstitutional.*

RAB-A-DAB-DAN

Rab-a-dab-dan, three men in the can,
And who might these gentlemen be?
Stephen Miller, Pompeo, and pale Jared Kushner
Who all screwed the pooch on TV.

As surrogates hawking the Dumpty agenda,
The three were unfortunate choices.
For starters, the public collectively cringed
At their smug oleaginous voices.

Dumpty let Miller creep out of his crypt
To go one-on-one with Jake Tapper.
He spouted saliva, invective, and venom
'Til Jake tossed him into the crapper.

As for Kushner, when Jonathan Swan took him on
He was stricken with waxen paralysis.
Questions on birthers, bin Salman, and such
Sent him reeling toward psychoanalysis.

But worst was the case of the plump Mike Pompeo
When harried by Mary Louise Kelly.
She wouldn't let up on Ukraine and Yovanovitch,
Sparking a sharp *casus belli*.

Right after, he lashed her with X-rated barbs,
Impugning her grasp of geography.
By reporting it dryly that evening on air,
Kelly tarnished Pompeo's biography.

Rab-a-dab-dan, three men in the can,
I think that we all can agree:
After laying an egg on occasions like these,
We won't see them much on TV.

STEPHEN MILLER, *senior advisor to Trump, appeared on* **JAKE TAPPER's** State of the Union *on January 7, 2018. As a result of Miller's hostile behavior, Tapper abruptly ended the interview and had Miller escorted off the CNN set.*

JARED KUSHNER, *Donald Trump's son-in-law and senior advisor, was interviewed by* **JONATHAN SWAN** *in season 2 of* Axios *on HBO and failed to answer questions on birtherism, refugees, Saudi Arabia, and his Middle East peace plan.*

MIKE POMPEO *became the secretary of state in April 2018. On January 24, 2020, he appeared on NPR's* All Things Considered *with* **MARY LOUISE KELLY,** *and an aide ended the interview early when Pompeo was asked about Ukraine.*

COUNSELOR JAY

The curious tale of Jay Sekulow
Is something he'd rather you didn't know.
A purveyor of right-wing political fictions,
His life is a web of bizarre contradictions
That arose at the outset when he was a boy:
A Brooklyn-born Jew but a Georgia-bred goy
Who embarked on his checkered professional journey
As Jews for Jesus's lead attorney.

But Jay had bigger fish to fry.
The media business had caught his eye.
As a red-meat Republican talking head,
His pocketbook was prodigally fed.
Once he'd made this venal choice,
He chucked his ethics and found his voice:
A strident libertarianism
Mashed up with evangelicalism.

Jay was on fire! Lady Fortune had found him!
Think tanks and charities sprang up around him.
Acronyms hawked his advocacy
Like the A-C-L-J and the C-L-A-G.
Hosannas were sung by Pat Robertson's throng
And the Fox punditocracy joined in the song.
Money sloshed in as his business took off
And a half dozen Sekulows slurped at the trough.

Yet as much as Jay cherished his growing empire,
He dreamed of the day when he'd climb even higher.
A national profile was out of his reach
As long as he languished in Virginia Beach.
But for Jay and his ilk, opportunity knocks
When President Dumpty spots you on Fox.
With POTUS afraid that the law would upend him,
He reached out to Jay to protect and defend him.

Thus it is we've come to know
Impeachment lawyer Sekulow.
Two years after his plum appointment
He's engineered King Dumpty's anointment,
Spooking the senatorial right
And smashing congressional oversight.
Craven hypocrisy had its day,
Stoked by the hokum of Counselor Jay.

Luxuriating in Dumpty's praise,
These are Sekulow's glory days.
But time is tough on shifty winners:
This year's saints are next year's sinners.
Fortune's fickle, rash, and cruel:
Dumpty's flack is fortune's fool.
When history deals its final blow,
Heaven help Jay Sekulow.

JAY SEKULOW *joined Donald Trump's legal team in 2017 and served as one of Trump's lead attorneys during the impeachment trial. Until the trial, Sekulow was best known for his fundraising on evangelical television and as a litigator for the Christian right, not for criminal law.*

TWINKLE, TWINKLE, KENNETH STARR

Twinkle, twinkle, Kenneth Starr,
Wonder how you passed the bar.
Doling out for all to see
Legalistic sophistry,
Twinkle, twinkle, Kenneth Starr,
Wonder how you passed the bar.

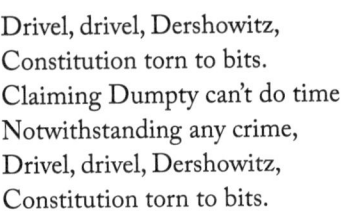

Drivel, drivel, Dershowitz,
Constitution torn to bits.
Claiming Dumpty can't do time
Notwithstanding any crime,
Drivel, drivel, Dershowitz,
Constitution torn to bits.

Bondi, Bondi won't recuse
Lest the president should lose.
Quashed her probe of Dumpty's grift
When he sent a campaign gift,
Bondi, Bondi won't recuse
Lest the president should lose.

Sneaky, sneaky Cipollone,
Well aware of quid pro quo-ny.
Heard about the scheme firsthand
In the room where it was planned,
Sneaky, sneaky Cipollone,
Well aware of quid pro quo-ny.

Sekulow and all his crew
Do what lackeys always do.
Ray, Purpura, Philbin, Raskin,
Dishing up what Dumpty's askin',
Just as slick as Kenneth Starr:
Wonder how they passed the bar.

The legal team for Donald Trump's impeachment trial in the Senate comprised several high-profile names, including **ALAN DERSHOWITZ,** *who had previously represented famous clients such as O. J. Simpson and Mike Tyson, and* **KENNETH STARR,** *the independent counsel whose investigation led to President Bill Clinton's impeachment in 1998.*

In 2013, Trump donated $25,000 to a group supporting the reelection of Florida attorney general **PAM BONDI,** *prompting suspicion that he was attempting to sway her office's review of fraud allegations against Trump University. Bondi was named part of Trump's impeachment defense team in January 2020.*

QUIET ELAINE

Deceptively sweet, the petite Elaine Chao
Hangs onto her power and no one knows how.
Where most of her cohorts have packed up and gone,
Quiet Elaine is still soldiering on.

With her easy allure, she's a breezy survivor.
Her sparkle disguises a DC conniver.
In Dumpty's dominion, it helps to be rich,
Not to mention her marriage to Senator Mitch.

Hoping to wangle a Cabinet pick,
Chao laid on the charm and she laid it on thick.
Of all the departments, she got Transportation:
A prime situation for bilking the nation.

In the agency henhouse, Elaine is the fox,
For example, her fistful of road-paving stocks.
In shipping as well, she is boss of all bosses.
Go figure: Her dad is a shipping colossus.

In Kentucky, the gifts from her family accounts
Pad Mitch's finances by staggering amounts.
But for brazen corruption, there's no greater case
Than the DOT traffic she steers to his base.

Survey the continent, search everywhere,
No man but McConnell exhibits less flare.
And yet with a boost from his spousal annuity
He bamboozles the government, in perpetuity.

Finding the perfect political wife
Is the best thing that happened to Mitch in his life.
A princess intent on extending her reign,
Watch your back when you're dealing with quiet Elaine.

ELAINE CHAO *assumed office as the U.S. secretary of trans-portation on January 31, 2017. When appointed, she failed to divest ownership of stock in Vulcan Materials, a construction and paving company that has received substantial funding from the Transportation Department. She sold her shares in June 2019. She is married to Senate Majority Leader Mitch McConnell and is the daughter of James Chao, founder of the Foremost Group, a New York–based shipping, trading, and finance company.*

BILL, BARR THE DOOR!

AG Barr, that faithful sentry,
Guards the Oval Office entry.
Though he stays all legal action,
He should check self-satisfaction:
Add a single scandal more
And he'll be frog-marched out the door.

WILLIAM "BILL" BARR *was appointed as the U.S. attorney general in February 2019. Though Barr had no official role in Trump's impeachment, he publicly defended the Trump administration on multiple occasions during and beyond the trials.*

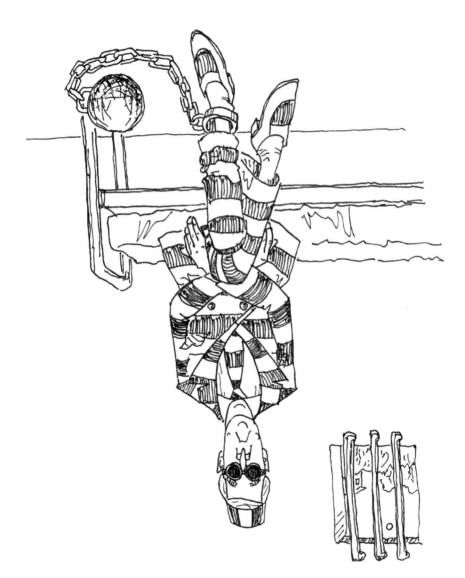

RUEFUL ROGER

A sentence was due for Rueful Roger,
Dirty trickster, artful dodger;
Hangdog dandy, glum and gaunt,
His trial had reached its denouement.

A year before in Lauderdale,
The feds hauled Roger off to jail.
The charges sent reporters scampering:
Obstruction, lies, and witness tampering.

Like the rest of Dumpty's crooks,
Roger hung on tenterhooks.
Doomed to reap what he had sown,
Fortune frowned on Roger Stone.

But aid and comfort from afar
Was smuggled in by William Barr.
The AG sneaked on from the sidelines,
Shortening Roger's sentencing guidelines.

Barr was certain none would notice
Favors for a friend of POTUS.
His cloak-and-dagger recommendation?
"Change nine years to mere probation!"

Roger crowed, although he saw
This clearly trashed the rule of law.
Waiting for the judge's sentence,
He smugly penned his fake repentance.

But just when all seemed hunky-dory,
Storm clouds darkened Roger's story:
Dumpty blabbed of Barr's intrusion
Stirring anger and confusion.

Four prosecutors cried "Disgrace!"
Threw a fit and quit the case;
Two thousand lawyers (ex-DOJ)
Demanded Barr be carted away.

The jig was up! The press discovered
A trail of dirt as yet uncovered:
Damning evidence to tar
Dumpty's bond with William Barr.

Thence the tale began to widen:
Attacks on Strzok, McCabe, and Biden,
Yet charges eased with wink and grin
For Rudy, Erik Prince, and Flynn.

An ugly truth came into focus:
POTUS and his hocus-pocus,
Bending justice to his ends,
Crushing foes and shielding friends.

A ruthless thug who dodged impeachment,
Emperor of over-reachment,
He'll try to dodge this bullet, too.
But honestly, what else is new?

This tale of justice run amok
Has claimed one hapless sitting duck.
Jail awaits its latest lodger,
Foolish, fallen persiflager,
Dirty trickster, artful dodger,
Not so artful . . .

Rueful Roger.

In January 2019, **ROGER STONE,** *a longtime Republican political strategist and Trump advisor, was arrested for witness tampering, obstructing an official proceeding, and making false statements about his foreknowledge of the release of Hillary Clinton's e-mails by WikiLeaks. He was found guilty of all seven charges brought against him, and in February 2020 federal prosecutors asked for a sentence of seven to nine years in prison. In an unprecedented development, the Department of Justice, led by William Barr, overruled the prosecutors' sentencing recommendation, and Stone received a forty-month sentence.*

OUR SUBSTITUTE
SCIENCE TEACHER

Mid-hurricane, Dumpty defied disbelief
With another bizarre aberration:
While Dorian doled out destruction and grief,
Alabama became his fixation.

He'd carelessly claimed just a few days before
That 'Bama should brace for a hit.
Contradicted by experts, he stamped on the floor
Storming out in a furious fit.

All week he was testy, defensive, and feral,
An angry and petulant harpy.
In the end, he provoked barometrical peril,
Defacing a map with a Sharpie.

At a time when the country was casting about
For a source of relief and reliance,
Instead all we got was a bilious lout
Substituting his Sharpie for science.

On September 1, 2019, Donald Trump announced the states that would be impacted by Hurricane Dorian and incorrectly included Alabama. On September 4, he showed reporters a weather map to defend his misstatement. It had been altered with a marker to show the hurricane's path threatening Alabama.

DUMPTY'S DOLLS

Dumpty's known to play with dolls
To put his restless mind at ease:
Pardon Power Action Figures
Modeled on his own grantees.

Take for instance Joe Arpaio,
Arizona's redneck cop:
Law defiler, race profiler,
Scourge of every traffic stop.

Dumpty's Scooter Libby doll
Is guaranteed to never squeal,
Plus providing reassurance
Perjury is no big deal.

His action figures often feature
Fraud, corruption, and deceit,
Like when Rod Blagojevich
Sells an empty Senate seat.

Or when the rich and prominent
Commit white-collar crime,
Like Kerik, Pogue, and Milken,
All renowned for doing time.

Dumpty plays with lady dolls
From several voting blocs:
Munoz, Hall, Negron, and Stanton
Fill the ballot box.

But *football* is a passion
Dumpty never will outgrow.
He'll while away the livelong day
With wee DeBartolo.

Dumpty weighs a hundred factors
Making pardon picks:
Friendly favors, shady money,
Underhanded politics.

But his main consideration,
Overriding all the rest:
He'll choose the worst offenders
So he'll always look the best.

Someday all of Dumpty's dolls
Will end up on the shelf.
On the evening news, you'll see
The latest Dumpty pardonee.
In the White House there he'll be,
Playing with himself.

Donald Trump has allegedly used his executive clemency powers on
controversial figures to reward friends, political allies, and donors.
Those pardoned or commuted include **JOE ARPAIO,** the former
sheriff and anti-illegal-immigration hardliner who was convicted
of contempt of court for disobeying a federal judge's order to stop
racial profiling; **ROD BLAGOJEVICH,** the former Illinois
governor who was sentenced to fourteen years in 2011 for trying
to peddle the Senate seat that Barack Obama vacated when elected
president; and **I. LEWIS "SCOOTER" LIBBY,** Vice President
Dick Cheney's former chief of staff, who was convicted of perjury
and obstruction of justice in 2007.

THE BUCKEYE FIRECRACKER

Jim Jordan, Buckeye Firecracker,
Dumpty's blindly loyal backer,
Struts through Congress, rash and raucous,
Bullhorn of the Freedom Caucus.
Sporting shirtsleeves, spewing spittle,
He pushed for POTUS's acquittal.
When it passed, he tossed his cap
And took a cocky victory lap.

But darker days bedevil Jim.
Karma may catch up with him.
Scandal has begun to brew
Around his years at OSU.
In a decade-long regime,
Jim co-coached their wrestling team.
By the time that he was done,
Ugly rumors had begun.

Grim reports of molestation
Scandalized the Buckeye Nation.
A dark, disquieting suspicion
Named the wrestling team's physician.
Jim's answer to his harried squad?
A craven wink and silent nod:
Toxic gossip, even though
It happened thirty years ago.

Jim Jordan, Buckeye Firecracker,
Ex-enforcer, ex-attacker,
Doberman who's lost his bite,
Nothing can relieve his plight.
The voice that stoked a thousand fears
Now falls on deaf, unheeding ears.
Jim's history has knocked him flat:
Hubris pinned him to the mat.

JIM JORDAN *is the Republican representative for the 4th district of Ohio and a former assistant coach of the Ohio State University wrestling team. He has been accused of ignoring charges against OSU's team physician, Dr. Richard Strauss, of sexual misconduct toward student wrestlers.*

TRUMPTY DUMPTY WANTED A ROUT

Trumpty Dumpty wanted a rout,
An electoral landslide to give him more clout.
With jobs and prosperity lending him fuel,
He wanted a lock on tyrannical rule.

With the dolorous Dems in a state of distress,
Dumpty could sense the sweet smell of success.
But in every good story, the plot always thickens:
The POTUS was careless in counting his chickens.

A gruesome pandemic assaulted the globe
Ironically hobbling our head germaphobe.
For when tragedy strikes of this harrowing scope,
It tends to expose a duplicitous dope.

Trumpty Dumpty was out on a limb.
His prospects of winning were suddenly dim.
Though history's verdict remains to be seen,
He's already a victim of COVID-19.

On January 22, 2020, Trump publicly downplayed the outbreak of COVID-19, stating, "We have it totally under control." By June, more than 100,000 Americans had died of the virus, and the percentage of unemployed workers hit its highest level since the Great Depression. Critics claimed that Trump's mismanagement of the pandemic response would cost him the 2020 election.

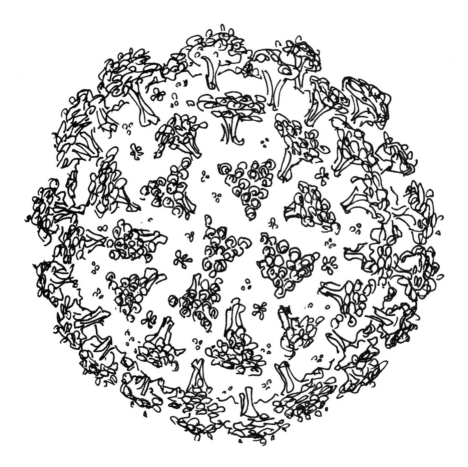

SCOUNDRELS AND HEROES: LIMERICKS FROM THE SEAT OF GOVERNMENT

Here follow some twenty-odd verses
On our national blessings and curses,
Each villain or hero
A Lincoln or Nero,
Reflecting our gains and reverses.

Scoundrels

1

At times, Dumpty's tortured with pain
From a history of too much Rogaine.
A tormenting prickle
Attacks his tes-tickle
When he glimpses the good ship *McCain.*

The files of McGahn and John Bolton
Hide corruption both crooked and joltin'.
But they never will tell
Lest their memoirs don't sell,
An embargo bizarre and revoltin'.

With the recent Rush Limbaugh disgrace,
Uncle Sam got a pie in the face.
POTUS opted to peddle
A crass Freedom Medal
To con his conservative base.

In a system that's hopelessly broken
The truth is infrequently spoken,
Suiting Rudy just fine
Since he's glad to align
With Lutsenko and Firtash and Shokin.

Lev Parnas and pal Igor Fruman
Were a duo whose business was boomin'.
As a fixer, each guy
Was the best you could buy
Which couldn't be said of their groomin'.

6

Intelligence Chair Richard Burr
Was a senator-entrepreneur.
Briefed on imminent shocks
He sold all of his stocks,
Then he hired a brand-new chauffeur.

7

Kelly Loeffler had barely begun
Her congressional time in the sun.
But her fortunes are fading
Since insider trading
Has put a swift end to her fun.

In the face of the coronavirus,
Dumpty's job was to cheer and inspire us.
The POTUS instead
Spread confusion and dread,
Since his secret desire was to fire us.

Ex-lobbyist Alex Azar,
An unlikely pandemical czar,
Was replaced by Mike Pence
Who's equally dense.
We continue to lower the bar.

10

The virus-denier Rand Paul
Displayed senatorial gall.
But then, to his shame,
He sadly became
The most toxic infector of all.

11

With all of his rallies suspended,
The POTUS felt lost and unfriended.
His briefings each day
Kept the demons at bay,
But our biodefense was upended.

12

A Cabinet man in too deep,
Ben Carson makes barely a peep.
By his droopy expressions
At Dumpty press sessions,
You'd think he was falling asleep.

13

When persuaded to take drastic actions,
Dumpty further divided our factions;
A perilous error
At moments of terror,
But worse are the coming attractions.

Heroes

14

House Intelligence chief Chairman Adam
Is a daredevil, tough as macadam.
The impeachment upheaval
Made him Evel Knievel.
We're awfully lucky we had 'm.

15

As diplomacy's classiest dame,
Yovanovitch merits that claim.
She's earned every honor.
May blessings rain on her
While Pompeo is mired in shame.

Colonel Vindman, the POTUS's nemesis,
Bears a fearlessness right out of Genesis.
Since he showed deeper fealty
Than our titan of realty,
Dumpty had him removed from the premises.

At her session on Capitol Hill,
Fiona was ready to spill.
When she rose to reveal
A shady drug deal,
Mick Mulvaney took suddenly ill.

18

Hearing Dumpty pugnaciously preach,
Nancy shredded the text of his speech.
She had to admit,
Having taken his shit,
Public trust was no day at the beach.

19

An impeachment so brazen and blistery
Made the absence of backbone a mystery.
Romney's boldness was stoic,
Heartfelt and heroic,
Placing Mitt on the right side of history.

20

Messonnier was a viral physician
With a high-minded medical mission.
Since to Dumpty the truth
Is corrupt and uncouth,
She was fated to lose her position.

21

Dr. Fauci, forced into the act,
Provided what Dumpty had lacked.
Reassurance at zero,
He emerged as a hero
While almost expiring from tact.

Coda

Vice and virtue has been our motif,
But virtue comes mostly to grief.
These verses on fakers
And crass mischief-makers
Mostly feature the Scoundrel in Chief.

Conservative radio host **RUSH LIMBAUGH** *received the 2020 Presidential Medal of Freedom despite his history of controversial and racist on-air comments.* **LEV PARNAS** *and* **IGOR FRUMAN**, *Rudy Giuliani's "fixers" during the Ukraine scandal, were charged with campaign finance violations. Senators* **RICHARD BURR** *and* **KELLY LOEFFLER** *sold major stocks just before the stock market plummet due to COVID-19. House Intelligence Committee chairman* **ADAM SCHIFF** *played a crucial role in the impeachment investigation against Trump. Former U.S. Ambassador* **MARIE YOVANOVITCH**, *Lieutenant Colonel* **ALEXANDER VINDMAN**, *and former U.S. National Security Council official* **FIONA HILL** *also gave testimonies during the impeachment. Republican senator* **MITT ROMNEY** *voted to convict Donald Trump on the first article of impeachment.*

A REQUIEM SCORED FOR KAZOO

Dumpty's farcical history with COVID-19
Is a requiem scored for kazoo.
It began years ago with his savage attacks
On Obama's response to swine flu.

Once elected as president, Dumpty cleaned house,
With Kushner, John Bolton, and Pence.
They abolished the office Obama created
To safeguard our biodefense.

They fired all the experts on microbes and viruses,
SARS and societal stress;
On testing, triage, vaccines, and containment.
But Dumpty? He couldn't care less.

Two years hence, at the end of Two Thousand Nineteen,
A discovery drew little notice:
A lethal new virus was spotted in China
And word was delivered to POTUS.

In the following weeks, every leader on earth
Was fixed upon care and prevention,
But not our distractible Tweeter in Chief.
Other matters took all his attention.

The virus struck Thailand, Japan, and Korea,
Spreading to zone after zone.
But Dumpty ignored it and focused instead
On the trial of his pal Roger Stone.

Italy caught it, the first Western nation,
Then Germany, Britain, and more;
While Dumpty perversely avenged his impeachment
By showing the Vindmans the door.

63

A case was detected in Washington State
Where our first major outbreak caught fire.
But a briefing on Russian electoral meddling
Drove Dumpty to sack Joe Maguire.

A Princess line cruiser with thousands on board
Was quarantined off Yokohama.
Dumpty's reaction? Downplay and deny,
With his usual swipe at Obama.

The global economy threatened to crater,
Potentially losing gazillions.
But at lush Mar-a-Lago, Dumpty played host
To a crowd of infected Brazilians.

Tom Hanks and wife Rita contracted the bug
As infections continued to soar,
While the prez sued the *Times*, CNN, and the *Post*
For reporting from nine months before.

Boris Johnson fell prey to the spreading contagion
As Britain lost billions of pounds.
Dumpty meanwhile flew to one of his clubs
To squeeze in a couple of rounds.

The virus mid-March had claimed thousands of lives
From hundreds of thousands of cases,
An appropriate moment for Dumpty to tweet
About Hillary's sundry disgraces.

At last an event captured Dumpty's attention,
A portent of mass ruination:
The stock market took a spectacular dive,
Demanding he speak to the nation.

In front of the camera, he sweated and squirmed,
A slug in a hypnotic trance.
Instead of a rally, the market collapsed,
With investors all crapping their pants.

Dumpty had finally gotten the drift,
Though it left him resentful and grouchy.
So our toddler POTUS turned over the mic
To a grown-up named Anthony Fauci.

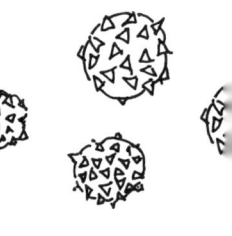

Thus ends Chapter One of a hair-raising saga
Of ignorance, lies, and privation;
A tale of confusion, contagion, and dread,
An oblivious leader in over his head,
And hope for more care and compassion ahead
In a healthier, happier nation.

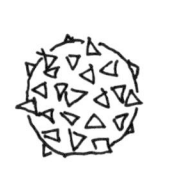

*On January 21, 2020, Washington State announced the first
U.S. case of coronavirus disease 2019 (COVID-19). In the
beginning stages of the outbreak, President Donald Trump and
his administration failed to take appropriate health and safety
precautions, despite the warnings of U.S. intelligence officials and*
DR. ANTHONY FAUCI, *the federal government's top infec-
tious disease expert.*

ONE LUCKY BASTARD

I'm one lucky bastard! I'm John McEntee!
A staffer as callow as callow can be!
From a preppie career as a star quarterback,
I followed my dream as a government hack.

With family pull, my ascendance began
When Dumpty made me his ace body man.
I never received my security clearance
But with Dumpty around, no one called interference.

John Kelly, that dick, threw me out on my can,
But it turned out the POTUS was my biggest fan.
With everyone else either fired or retiring,
He hired me as head of all hiring and firing.

Keeping my job is as easy as pie:
I make sure all appointees are dumber than I.
Their job application is simple to pass,
A promise to constantly kiss Dumpty's ass.

Everyone tells me I'm doing just fine,
And who would've figured? I'm just twenty-nine!
I'm a staffer as callow as callow can be!
I'm one lucky bastard! I'm John McEntee!

JOHN MCENTEE, *who was known for making a viral football video and had worked in social media at Fox News, was hired as Donald Trump's personal assistant in 2016. He was fired by Chief of Staff* **JOHN KELLY** *in 2018 over allegations of security clearance and finance issues. Within twenty-four hours, he was hired as the senior advisor for Trump's campaign operations. In 2020, he was promoted to director of the Presidential Personnel Office, where his role is to identify and replace staffers suspected of disloyalty to the president.*

THE SPECIAL OPS OF ERIK PRINCE

The special ops of Erik Prince
Can make you wince.

A name invoking random slaughter,
That's Blackwater.

Defense contractor profiteer,
That's his career.

Privatizing foreign wars,
His fortune soars.

The massacre in Nisour Square,
His men were there.

Meddling in South Sudan,
He's your man.

Skulduggery in far Seychelles,
He never tells.

Stings for Project Veritas,
Bet your ass.

Hired by POTUS, Flynn, and Bannon,
Another loose cannon.

Ace of heinous sleight of hand,
Dumpty's word is his command.
He executes that dark agenda
Like the Prisoner of Zenda.

Mayhem's dirty fingerprints,
That's Erik Prince.

ERIK PRINCE, *founder of the private military company Blackwater Worldwide, has served as an informal advisor to the Trump administration. In recent years, Prince allegedly helped recruit former spies for operations that included infiltrating Democratic congressional campaigns and other groups considered hostile to the Trump agenda.*

DIPLOMATIC GAS

Mike Pompeo's pungent flatus
Tends to make our allies hate us.
Once, he made an awful stink
On G7's interlink.
Disputing their collective statement
On pandemical abatement,
Mike put up inflexible resistance
Overwhelming social distance.
He fixed the blame for the infection,
Claiming a Chinese connection.
"Simple facts," he cried, "require us
To title it 'The Wuhan Virus'!"
All the ministers objected.
Mike's pronouncement was rejected.
No statement was released at all
Due to Mike Pompeo's gall.
Such a stunt, we know full well,
Leaves behind an awful smell.
If they hadn't been on Zoom,
Pompeo would have cleared the room.

On March 25, 2020, a G7 meeting was held over videoconference amidst the spreading coronavirus. Since the virus was first reported in Wuhan, China, Secretary of State Mike Pompeo insisted on calling it "the Wuhan virus." The WHO, Chinese officials, and other world leaders advised against it.

RECIPE FOR DISASTER

Try a viral new cuisine,
COVID-19.

Offer it to each civilian
(Three hundred million).

It's quick and easy to prepare
Microbial fare.

First preheat an anxious nation
With misinformation.

Take what other leaders tried
And set aside.

Place the fifty sovereign states
On separate plates.

Sow confusion and distrust,
Make your crust.

Insist on sycophantic praise,
Whip the glaze.

Stir the pot for all to see
On live TV.

Add DeSantis, simmer low,
Cuomo? No.

Pound Jay Inslee, call him snake,
Then prebake.

Claim it's Gretchen Whitmer's fault,
Pinch of salt.

If the kitchen is a mess,
Slam the press.

If the pastry comes unstuck,
Pass the buck.

Are supplies arriving late?
Blame the state.

Shuck all science-based advice,
Puree twice.

If the Stock Exchange careens,
Boil your greens.

For a dash of ignorance,
Add Mike Pence.

Use your clueless son-in-law
For the slaw.

Slash the funds for WHO,
Knead the dough.

Add some spice to this fiasco
With Tabasco.

Once you learn how it can kill,
Throw in dill.

When a hundred thousand die,
Bake your pie.

When at last the horror's done,
Claim you won.

Takes no time at all to master
National disaster.

While COVID-19 was spreading rapidly and killing scores of Americans, Donald Trump and his administration continued to downplay the pandemic and spread misinformation, ignore the warnings of international leaders, and unconstitutionally challenge the authority of local governors.

REETLE-DEET-DEET

Reetle-deet-deet, two men of the fleet,
Run aground on a perilous reef:
Captain Brett Crozier and Thomas B. Modly,
Brought down by the Bungler in Chief.

At the onset of COVID, Captain Crozier's ship
Had five thousand sailors on board.
Alerting the brass to the risk of infections,
His warning was blithely ignored.

A leak to the press of the Captain's distress
Made Navy Chief Modly irate.
Dreading the usual Dumpty eruption,
He quickly showed Crozier the gate.

A top-flight commander's demotion and slander
Came off like a hydrogen bomb,
Enraging the Navy and public alike
And dispatching poor Modly to Guam.

He spoke to the crew on the vessel's PA,
A harangue full of Dumptyan blather.
His intent was to calm, reassure, and explain,
But his rant left them all in a lather.

A tape of his tirade was Modly's demise,
He resigned amid damning critiques.
Irony hung in the seafaring air:
Two Navy men scuppered by leaks.

Reetle-deet-deet, two men of the fleet,
Tarnished heroes of fading renown.
In service to Dumpty's chaotic command,
Alas, they were destined to drown.

On March 30, 2020, **CAPTAIN BRETT CROZIER** *sent an e-mail to ten Navy officers pleading for a quick evacuation of his ship, the USS* Theodore Roosevelt, *to prevent the spread of the coronavirus on board. The letter was leaked to the* San Francisco Chronicle, *and on April 2, 2020, Crozier was relieved of his command by acting Navy Secretary* **THOMAS MODLY.** *Modly resigned shortly after amid public outrage over his mishandling of the COVID-19 crisis aboard the ship and his criticism of Crozier.*

FIRE BRIGHT!

Here's a tale of shock and spite,
Of dread disease and petty spite,
About a man whose stand was right
Yet suffered Dumpty's rabid bite.

Heightening our COVID plight
And coming off as Putin-lite,
The POTUS wielded reckless might
And fired virologist Rick Bright.

A clinician with astute insight
Whose rep was solidly airtight,
Rick spurned the role of weak, contrite,
And sycophantic acolyte.

Our presidential troglodyte,
Spoiling for a nasty fight,
Ousted Bright in dead of night
(While staying safely out of sight).

The root of Dumpty's vengeful sin?
Alas, hydroxychloroquine.

RICK BRIGHT *was abruptly dismissed in April 2020 as the director of the Department of Health and Human Services' Biomedical Advanced Research and Development Authority, the federal agency involved in developing a coronavirus vaccine. He had pressed for careful vetting of off-label use of the anti-malaria drug hydroxychloroquine, which President Trump had been pro-moting as a treatment for COVID-19.*

THE INVISIBLE MAN

My name is Brad Parscale, I do what I can.
I'm Dumpty's essential Invisible Man.
I've been at his side since the very creation,
His maestro of media disinformation.
I'm the towering Texan who made him the POTUS,
Yet I constantly strive to escape public notice.
My political mantra I chant by the hour:
Work in the dark when you're wielding dark power.

When Dumpty gears up for another election,
My impact is felt like a viral infection.

I launch all my strategies, plots, and schemata
By harvesting truckloads of voters' raw data
Then clog up the Web with my Internet litter
On Facebook and Instagram, TikTok and Twitter.
Millions are lured by my grand master plan
Since no one can see the Invisible Man.

When the story is told of King Dumpty's ascendance,
My name will appear in the very first sentence.
His fiery climb was a walk in the park:
He provided the fuel, I provided the spark.
When I threw my dust in America's eye,
You couldn't distinguish a fact from a lie,
You couldn't distinguish the bad from the good:
The Invisible Man did all that he could.

While serving as the digital media director for Donald Trump's
2016 presidential campaign, **BRAD PARSCALE** collected voters'
raw data to craft a powerful and lucrative digital campaign. He
was hired as the campaign manager for Trump's 2020 reelection
effort.

A PANDEMIC'S A TERRIBLE THING TO WASTE

1

For a desperate POTUS, impeached and disgraced,
A pandemic's a terrible thing to waste.
Hence with markets a bust and the virus let loose,
Dumpty put COVID-19 to good use.

With the country in quarantine, fretful and nervous,
He decided to hit the intelligence service.
So late on a Friday, behind all our backs,
He gave their Inspector General the ax.

This was Michael K. Atkinson, you may recall,
Who had taken bold action the preceding fall
By reporting a whistleblower's secret complaint
Portraying the POTUS as less than a saint.

Thus driven by malice and base retribution,
Dumpty subverted a key institution.
He lowered the boom with the nation asleep
And because of the virus, we heard not a peep.

2

With another IG, he took the same line
When the following week he evicted Glenn Fine,
In charge of emergency dollars and cents
That Dumpty appointed himself to dispense.

When next he fell prey to his dissatisfaction,
HHS was the setting for more covert action.
Seized by a petty, misogynist whim,
He ousted their acting IG, Christi Grimm.

Mitch Behm, the ex-Transportation IG,
Fourth target of POTUS's firing spree,
Got the noose for refusing to bend or kowtow
In unearthing the dirt on the pert Elaine Chao.

But worst was the fate of the IG from State,
Steve Linick, served up with his head on a plate.
With the pathogen panicking most of the nation,
There was barely a word of his defenestration.

In sum, *five inspectors* were given the can
As Dumpty pursued his nefarious plan.
In the midst of a violent viral eruption,
No one was left to inspect his corruption.

LES INSPECTEURS GENERALES DE CALAIS

3

In building a modern American monarchy,
Dumpty's best tool is pandemical anarchy.
Look closely. You'll spot several instances more
Of Dumpty the King with his foot in the door:

Live daily briefings of rash volatility
Consigning his rivals to invisibility;
Demagoguery polished to toxic perfection
Inciting his backers to armed insurrection;

Bashing China for blatant political gain;
Reinforcing his anti-asylum campaign;
Upending science with lies in his throat;
Screwing the governors and skewing the vote.

As fatalities mount and hysteria rages,
These stories get bumped to the very back pages,
A scheme by which Dumpty can slyly obscure
The shocking mistakes of a bungling boor.

4

Thus the crisis we thought was most apt to expose him
May instead make it futile to ever depose him.
He's rendered democracy weak and debased:
A pandemic's a terrible thing to waste.

In April and May 2020, while the COVID-19 pandemic raged, Trump fired four inspectors general in his executive branch:

MICHAEL ATKINSON, *inspector general of the intelligence community, who had given to Congress the whistleblower complaint that led to Trump's impeachment;*

CHRISTI GRIMM, *acting inspector general of the Department of Health and Human Services, who had reported delayed test results and widespread shortages of medical supplies such as masks and testing kits;*

MITCH BEHM, *acting inspector general of the Department of Transportation, who had begun looking into Secretary Elaine Chao's dealings with the state of Kentucky; and*

STEVE LINICK, *inspector general of the State Department, who had been investigating alleged abuses of power at the department.*

In addition, **GLENN FINE** *was removed as head of the Pandemic Response Accountability Committee overseeing $2 trillion in emergency relief aid. Two weeks later, he resigned as the acting inspector general of the Defense Department.*

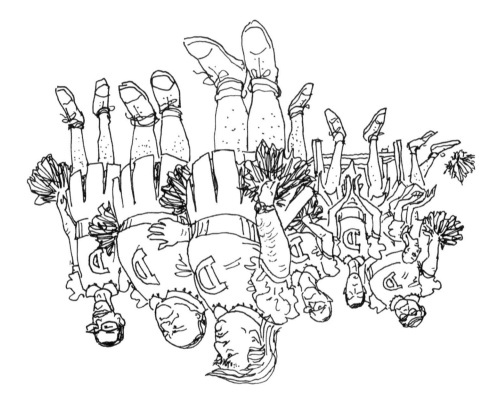

RAH! RAH! RAH!

(The head cheerleader exhorts the squad to sell his policies to an anxious public)

Kushner! Kushner! He's our man!
If he can't do it, Miller can!

Miller! Miller! He's our man!
If he can't do it, Kudlow can!

Kudlow! Kudlow! He's our man!
If he can't do it, Mnuchin can!

Mnuchin! Mnuchin! He's our man!
If he can't do it, Barr can!

Barr! Barr! He's our man!
If he can't do it, Pompeo can!

Pompeo! Pompeo! He's our man!
If he can't do it, Kayleigh can!

Kayleigh! Kayleigh! She's all heart!
The only one who looks the part!

Pearly teeth and golden tan!
If she can't do it, TEAM can!

Team! Team! Too damn tired!
If they can't do it, *they get fired*!

At a coronavirus briefing on March 31, 2020, Donald Trump called himself "a cheerleader for the country." Despite polls showing decreasing support for Trump's handling of the coronavirus, the Trump administration continued to praise the president's response, boast of false successes, and hype new policies amidst the pandemic.

KAYLEIGH MCENANY *was appointed as Trump's fourth press secretary in April 2020. She joined a communications office that has experienced frequent turnover under Trump.*

THE TORYS,
OR THE TIGER KING

Take a moment to pity the poor GOP,
They're as lost and confused as a party can be.
Inspired by their recent calamitous stories,
Here's a family fable: We'll call it "The Torys."

1

Generations had passed but the Torys endured,
A Washington family, proud and assured.
Their forebears had left them with money and power:
Reagan, the Bushes, and Dwight Eisenhower.

The family's children were lively and sweet,
The corridors rang with their pattering feet.
Playing one day near the Capitol dome,
They found a stray kitten and carried him home.

For the children, the kitten was fun and exciting
In spite of his penchant for scratching and biting.
His flushed orange face and his lackluster eyes
Foreshadowed a life of corruption and lies.

But the kids didn't care! They wanted to claim him.
They angrily fought about what they should name him:
"Whiskers" or "Tabby," "Grimalkin" or "Pi."
They settled on "Dumpty" (though heaven knows why).

The parents and grandparents sternly resisted.
The children all pouted and loudly insisted.
The grown-ups relented, resolving the spat,
Unaware they'd adopted a wild tiger cat.

2

With feline ferocity marking his essence,
The tiger grew up to a fierce adolescence.
Snappish and lumbering, cocky and cruel,
The Torys dispatched him to military school.

Though in college he managed to pick up some breeding,
The cat never bothered with writing or reading.
No surprises: In spite of his Ivy degree,
The brain of a tiger's the size of a pea.

Launching himself in the family biz,
Dumpty was hailed as a real estate whiz.
Though tending to swindle, to cheat, and to bungle,
A tiger will thrive by laws of the jungle.

His carnivorous hunger for animal pleasures
Brought him an empire of assets and treasures:
Casinos and golf courses, hotels and clubs,
Three different spouses and five tiger cubs.

A reality show was the next on his tray
Where his bright orange stripes were on constant display.
His brand had transcended mere real estate czar:
He was Dumpty the Tiger! A media star!

3

Fame having stirred Dumpty's feline ambition,
He sharpened his claws for a daring new mission:
Egged on by the animals held in his thrall,
He would campaign for POTUS the following fall.

The Torys reacted with horror and shame
At the thought of a tiger disgracing their name.
Fearing the likes of a dozen Fort Sumters,
They formed an alliance of staunch Never-Dumpters.

At first they sought out a political savior
To counter their tiger's rapacious behavior.
But no matter how stoutly his rivals would strive,
In primary season, he ate them alive.

Dumpty's campaigning was ruthless and shady.
His electoral foe was a former first lady.
Sane and familiar (and female at that),
She was juicy red meat for a ravenous cat.

Having cravenly failed to derail or unhorse him,
The Torys were finally forced to endorse him.
Despite how he made them all tremble and cower,
They decided at last they would ride him to power.

Civility, justice, and reason took wing
As Dumpty was crowned the supreme Tiger King.
Then with murderous appetite, savage and hearty,
He ate every soul in the Grand Tory Party.

4

There's a moral I urge you to never forget
To this frightening fable (that's not over yet):
If you coddle a tiger and venture to ride him,
You're certain, dear reader, to end up inside him.

In the American Revolution, a "Tory" was a subject who remained loyal to the British Crown. Today, the word has become shorthand for members of the conservative party in Canada and the United Kingdom.

Despite the opposition of several prominent Republican officials, Donald Trump emerged as the Republican presidential nominee in 2016. His nomination followed decades of party tension, the growth of conservative media, a divided Congress, and a muddled political landscape with no clear GOP leader.

On March 20, 2020, Netflix premiered the eight-part documentary series Tiger King. *It proved to be a major hit.*

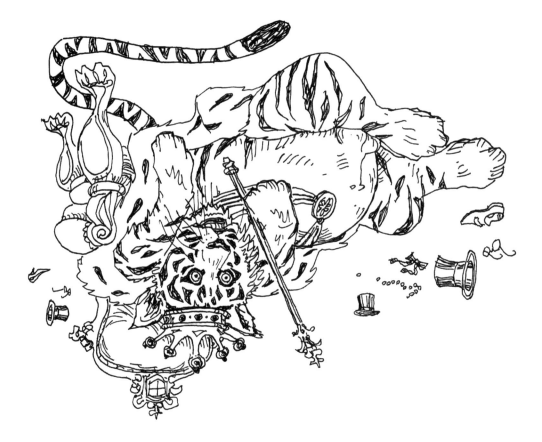

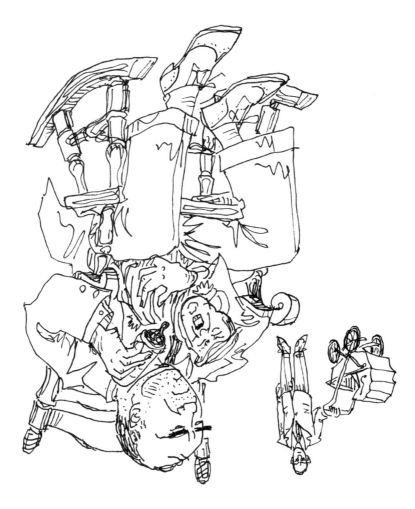

JOE MCCARTHY'S LULLABY

Hush, little Dumpty, don't you cry,
You'll be in dreamland by and by.

Harken back many years ago
To the time of your Uncle Joe.

If you're feeling all alone,
Give a thought to Roy M. Cohn.

If you're cranky, be like me:
Copy my demagoguery.

Stoke the nation's tribal schism
By attacking socialism.

Crap on legal jurisdiction
By rescinding Flynn's conviction.

If you hype the Chinese connection,
You'll squeak by in the next election.

If your polls are getting low,
Implicate Joe Scarborough.

You can win every crucial state
By invoking Obamagate.

If you're badly trailing Biden,
Claim you know everything he's hidin'.

If they call you "deeply flawed,"
Keep invoking voter fraud.

If coronavirus spreads,
Put it all on the governors' heads.

If they claim you reacted slow,
Place the blame on the WHO.

If resistance grows too large,
Float the bogus Deep State charge.

If the public feels chagrin,
Tout hydroxychloroquine.

If at last you're voted down,
You'll still be the sweetest little Dumpty in town.

So hush little Dumpty, don't you cry,
You're out of office by and by.

In the 1950s, Wisconsin senator **JOSEPH MCCARTHY,** *along with his chief counsel* **ROY M. COHN,** *investigated suspected communists in U.S. government and society. His reckless tactics spawned the term "McCarthyism." Years later, Cohn acted as Donald Trump's attorney and mentor.*

On May 7, 2020, William Barr's Justice Department dropped the criminal case against Trump's former national security advisor **MICHAEL T. FLYNN** *for lying to the FBI, despite his having twice pleaded guilty to the charge.*

Five days later, Trump claimed on Twitter that MSNBC's **JOE SCARBOROUGH** *may have "[gotten] away with murder" in the accidental death of his former aide Lori Klausutis nineteen years before.*

OUR WITCH DOCTOR IN CHIEF

Dumpty suggests disinfectant injections
To save us from COVID's pernicious infections,
Or a frontal attack to defeat it outright
By blasting our lungs with salubrious light.
A blithering idiot, gone round the bend:
When in the world will this lunacy end?

During a White House coronavirus task force briefing on April 23, 2020, President Donald Trump suggested using ultraviolet light and injecting disinfectants into the body to help fight the coronavirus.

TRUMPTY DUMPTY
WANTED A TITLE

Trumpty Dumpty wanted a title.
To him, an imperious handle was vital:
Dumpty the Bold or Dumpty the Great,
A moniker lending his legacy weight.

He tortured his brain for a suitable label:
Dumpty the Genius or Dumpty the Stable,
Dumpty the Wise or perhaps the Sublime
(Not Dumpty the Orange: It's too hard to rhyme).

While urgent emergencies went unaddressed,
An appropriate nickname had Dumpty obsessed.
But given what's passed and what's yet to befall him,
History will shortly decide what to call him.

A POTUS whose pants are routinely on fire
Could be Dumpty the Huckster or Dumpty the Liar.
With his bullshit throughout our pandemic attack,
An apt nom de guerre would be Dumpty the Quack.

With electoral help he's received from afar,
There's Dumpty the Russian or Dumpty the Czar.
Racial intolerance? Open the spigot
For the odious record of Dumpty the Bigot.

Daddy's podiatrist helped him defer,
Hence Dumpty the Bone and Dumpty the Spur.
Take his prurient past and, for accuracy's sake,
Call him Dumpty the Lecher or Dumpty the Rake.

The scandals and crimes that have always erupted
Make him Dumpty the Venal, Malign, or Corrupted.
Compared to the others, going back to the first,
Whatever you name him, he's Dumpty the Worst.

What title can conjure
This ludicrous gent,
A POTUS who hastened
A nation's descent?
At the end of this age
Of profound discontent,
I'll settle for Dumpty

The Ex-President.

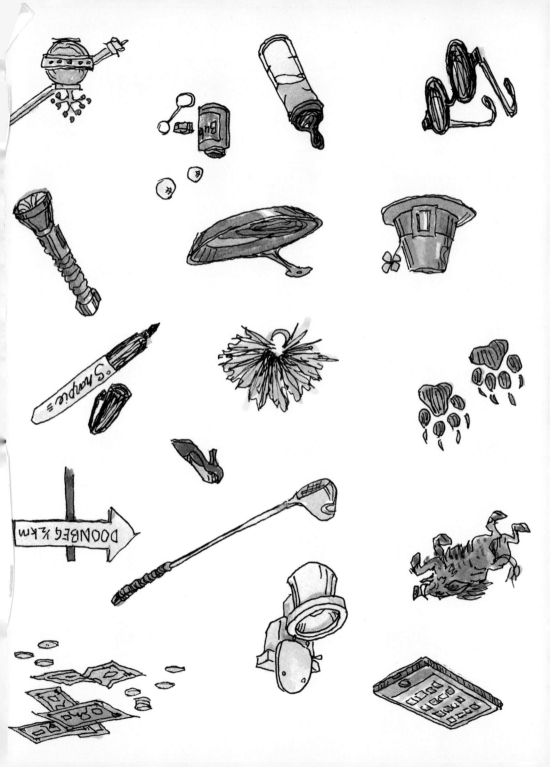